il Cenacolo

Guide to the Refectory

il Cenacolo

Pietro C. Marani

Guide to the Refectory

Electa

Cover illustration
Leonardo, Last Supper, *detail, Milan,*
Refectory of Santa Maria delle Grazie

Translation by Margaret Kunzle
and Felicity Lutz for Scriptum, Rome

This volume was published by Electa, Milan
Elemond Editori Associati

Contents

Forward to the Second Edition

Over twenty years after the beginning of the restoration work, Leonardo's *Last Supper* has been returned to the international world of culture and the public eye in a state of preservation that perhaps it has never been possible to achieve since the sixteenth century. At the beginning of the extremely delicate restoration process we did not have the intention, or labour under the illusion, of bringing back to light Leonardo's painting exactly as Leonardo had left it after putting down his brush for the last time. But we aimed, above all, to conserve the original layers of colour that still − we were certain − had survived the five centuries of its tormented history, and the quality and quantity of what we found far exceeded our expectations. The painting, however, comes down to us in an altered and distorted form, not only because of the length of time that has passed and the vicissitudes it has undergone, but because of past critical readings and interpretations of it, because of the copies made of it, and, last but not least, because of the image of it that has become familiar to the collective memory. Thus, while the fragments unveiled by this restoration still display their age and the "signs" of the time that has passed (which could be described as the historical significance of the painting), the visitor has to make a great effort to link this newly restored work to the "idea" imprinted in his mind (through the numerous popular reproductions and photographs in circulation, which are all touched up and altered to give as complete an image as possible of the picture). The painting is certainly fragmentary, since there are large areas where nothing of the original survives. However, the fragments with their intense, bright colours, linked together by very meticulous, thinner, water-colour additions (so that it is always evident where the original painting finishes and where the areas in which it has been lost begin) now contribute to creating a more reliable image and one that is closer to the lost original than the eighteenth-century repaintings. Apart from altering and distorting the faces, expressions, attitudes and colours, they had also concealed the general effect of the composition for over two centuries, by removing any suggestion of depth, and, above all, by eliminating the extremely balanced play of light and shadow, which today gives the fragmentarily rediscovered painting the tonal equilibrium that Leonardo had used to solve the problem of the relation between chiaroscuro and colour.

In reprinting this text almost fifteen years after it was first published, I have not wanted to alter the content, because this is intended to be a first historically orientated approach to the appreciation and understanding of this famous mural painting. The whole of the first part (which attempts to reconstruct its history and significance) is therefore little changed, whereas it has been necessary to make some corrections and additions to the last part, where the results of the restoration – then in progress and now completed – are referred to. Given that this demanding restoration work was also affected by the duration of the process, and there were noticeable changes in direction and methodology (though the high quality of philological research that had inspired it from the outset was always maintained), which are reflected in the accounts and studies that have accompanied the restoration, a bibliography has been added so that the interested reader can obtain further information. One of the material aspects that the restoration has definitively confirmed, by very recently re-examining the stratigraphy, concerns, for example, the type of medium Leonardo employed. The chemical and physical analyses conducted on samples of paint have established beyond any reasonable doubt that tempera was used, perhaps with a thin layer of oil in some places, on two layers of plaster. From the standpoint of the perspective scheme adopted by Leonardo, the rediscovery of the lines he cut in the upper left portion of the composition, and the definitive reading of the band on the extreme right after the first tapestry as part of a wall depicted in perspective, have confirmed that the artist reproduced an imaginary room wider than the actual Refectory, in order to suggest a more scenographic, illusionistic background from which the table and the figures of Christ and the apostles emerge three-dimensionally.

P.C.M.

Plan of Santa Maria delle Grazie and Its Refectory with the *Last Supper*

Key

I   Entrance to the *Last Supper*

II   Large Cloister

III   Refectory with the *Last Supper*

IV   Church of Santa Maria delle Grazie

①   Leonardo, *Last Supper*

②   Donato Montorfano, *Crucifixion*

Services

Ⓐ   *reception and ticket office*

Ⓑ   *toilets*

Ⓒ   *bookshop*

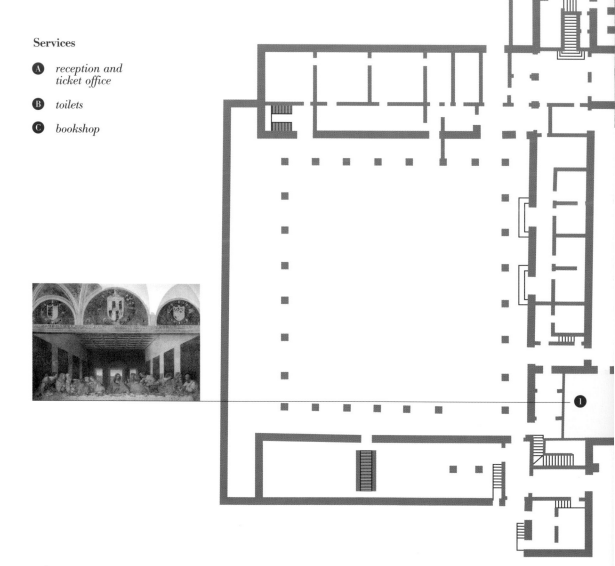

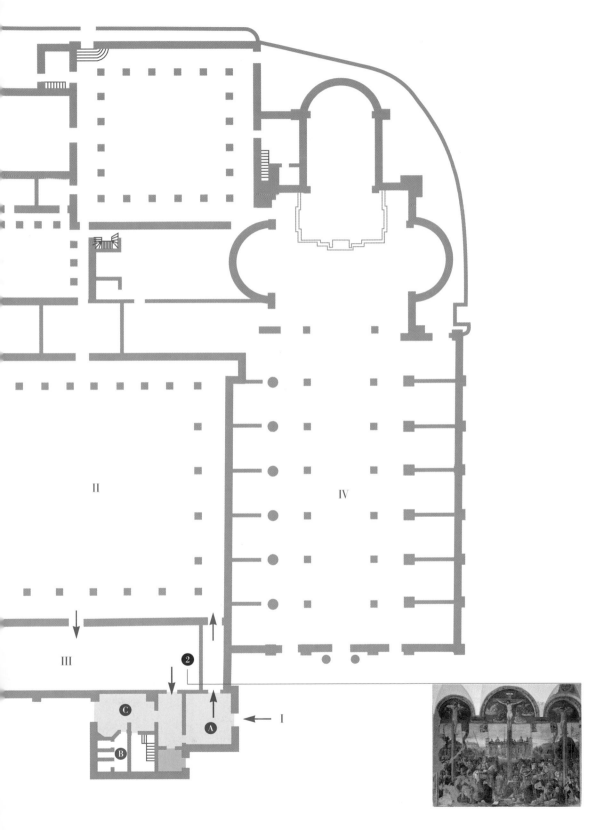

Leonardo's *Last Supper*

Pietro C. Marani

Interior of the refectory of the church of Santa Maria delle Grazie

The refectory damaged by bombing in August 1943

A sheet preserved in the Royal Library at Windsor Castle, no. 12542r, illustrates Leonardo's early ideas for the *Last Supper*, or *Cenacolo*, in Santa Maria delle Grazie.[1] It shows five figure studies; the largest, at the top of the sheet, represents eight or nine disciples grouped around Christ, with Judas seated on the near side of the table. The scene is set against a wall along which run the corbels of a vault, creating a row of lunettes, just as in the real architecture of the long walls of the Refectory of the Grazie (although there is no reason to think that Leonardo intended to paint the *Cenacolo* on one of these walls — the figures would in fact have been enormous).

The drawing, done with lively, darting pen strokes, is deliberately concise: the features of the heads are barely indicated by blots and crossed dashes marking the brow lines and noses. The second drawing, on the right hand side of the sheet, is on a slightly larger scale and shows the group of Christ, John, Peter and Judas as described in the Gospel of Saint John (13, 21–26): "When Jesus had thus said, he was troubled in spirit, and testified, and said, 'Verily, verily, I say unto you, that one of you shall betray me.' Then the disciples looked one on another, doubting of whom he spake. Now there was leaning on Jesus' bosom one of his disciples, whom Jesus loved. Simon Peter therefore beckoned to him, that he should ask who it would be of whom he spake. He then lying on Jesus' breast saith unto him, 'Lord, who is it?' Jesus answered, 'He it is, to whom I shall give a sop, when I have dipped it.' And when he had dipped the sop, he gave it to Judas Iscariot, the son of Simon."

Leonardo therefore initially chose to portray the moment which had already been represented by artists for centuries, when Christ gives the sop of bread to Judas, thus identifying him as the traitor. As Jack Wasserman has pointed out, among the first portrayals of this episode described by Saint John (in the Gospel according to Saint Luke, the traitor is identified by his hands, which are with Christ's on the table, a scene apparently never painted) there is a relief in the cathedral of Volterra; another, dating from the twelfth century, in San Giovanni Fuoricivitas at Pistoia; and a fres-

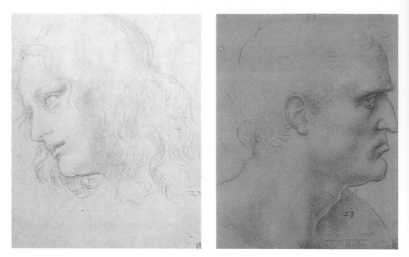

Leonardo, Study for the head of James the Greater. Windsor Castle, Royal Collection (no. 12552)

Leonardo, Study for the head of Philip. Windsor Castle, Royal Collection (no. 12551)

Leonardo, Head in profile facing right. Windsor Castle, Royal Collection (no. 12548)

Leonardo (with later repainting), Head of Christ. Milan, Pinacoteca di Brera

co of the same century in the abbey of Viboldone, just outside Milan.[2]

But the most striking feature of Leonardo's drawing is the extraordinary detail of Christ's left arm presented in two positions: one outstretched, in the act of taking or handing the bread, and the other withdrawn, in the gesture of pointing or moving towards the plate. This creates a sort of photographic sequence which gives the scene vitality and movement. Added to this there is the reaction of Saint Peter, who shows astonishment and stares at Judas with a severe, questioning look, moving his hand to his forehead. His expression contrasts with that of Christ, who already appears suffering, merciful and resigned. It is quite extraordinary how Leonardo, with a few pen strokes and blots, in a few square centimetres of paper, could concentrate such a great variety of attitudes, movements, expressions and meanings. This makes us regret all the more that much of the great mural has been lost. In the painting, the subtle variations, correspondences and resonances between one character and another must have been much more marked. The Windsor sheet is therefore all the more important, and certainly the most significant among the surviving studies for the painting.[3]

Another series of preliminary remarks suggests itself before we go on to consider Leonardo's masterpieces itself. The sheet discussed here, Windsor 12542, besides other figure drawings connected with the *Cenacolo*, both on the *recto* and the *verso* presents several studies relating to architecture, geometry and mechanics. These drawings confirm the date of the sheet, around 1492–94, and are interesting because they link the studies for the *Cenacolo*, and the painting itself, to a particular period of Leonardo's activity marked by an especially wide range of interests and studies. This was the decade 1490–99, one of the most busy and

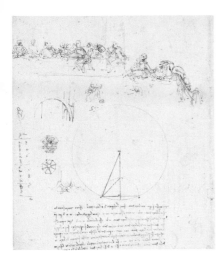

Leonardo, Studies for the Last Supper. Windsor Castle, Royal Collection (no. 12542)

stimulating for Leonardo. Besides his work as an artist, in those years he devoted himself particularly to the study of movement and mechanical phenomena, while also elaborating observations and notes which he hoped would develop into a consistent, organic treatise on painting. The result of his studies of mechanics, ballistics, the repercussion of movements, visual rays and sound, and of anatomy as a system of mechanics applied to the human body, is already clear in the Windsor drawing 12542r and is fully reflected in the *Cenacolo*.

In the painting, however, the moment of the Passion which is represented is not the one illustrated in the preparatory studies of the Windsor sheet. We have no documentation of Leonardo's transition from this initial stage, but the moment represented in the mural is the one immediately preceding the identification of Judas, when Christ makes the statement: "One of you shall betray me." These words evoke immediate astonishment and an emotional reaction in the apostles. Peter turns to John inviting him to question Jesus, just as described in the verses from Saint John's Gospel quoted above (and in fact John, rather than lying on Jesus' breast as in the traditional representations of the Last Supper, is sitting back, because Peter has called on him to ask Christ for an explanation). Christ's words, "One of you shall betray me," strike the apostles like sound waves, rebounding from one to another and creating the variety of their gestures, attitudes and movements. It is as though the diagram of a law of acoustics, optics and dynamics[4] had been directly translated into painting. The different reactions of the apostles correspond to the different ways a light ray is reflected and returns, according to the type of surface refracting it. This is confirmed by certain observations of Leonardo's. In particular, there are two passages in a manuscript entirely devoted to problems of light and shade, the Institut de France Ms. C, f. 16r, dating from around 1490, in which Leonardo compares the diffusion of sound and visual rays: "On reflected movements. I desire to define why bodily and spiritual movements, after striking the object rebound at equal angles.

On bodily movements. I say the re-echoing voice is reflected by striking the ear, as objects striking mirrors are reflected to the eye. And just as the image falls from the thing to the mirror and from the mirror to the eye at an equal angle, so the voice, when it first strikes the ear, will fall and rebound at equal angles in the cavity."

Other notes comparing the propagation of sound to that of visual rays, and likening these effects to the diffusion of waves around a point struck in water, can also be found in manuscripts almost entirely devoted to problems of paint-

Leonardo, Study for the hands of John. Windsor Castle, Royal Collection (no. 12543)

ing. They appear, for example, in sheets 9v and 19v of the Paris Ms. A, 1490–92 circa; and also Ms. H, sheet 67r[5] and in an older sheet, dating from around 1490, of the *Codex Atlanticus*, 1041r (ex f. 373r-b), which presents the following conclusions: "The stone, where it strikes the surface of the water, causes circles around it which spread until they are lost; and in the same way the air, struck by a voice or a noise, also has a circular motion, so that he who in nearest hears it best and he who is most distant cannot hear it." These words seem to be a literal illustration of the attitudes of the disciples around Christ.

In approaching the *Last Supper*, then, we should also consider the related studies in optics, mechanics and dynamics which occupied Leonardo in the immediately preceding period and during the years when he was working on the painting. The perspectival plan is very much in evidence, but his extreme simplicity in fact conceals another key for understanding the painting. The composition even suggests that circular form which Leonardo always loved as life-propelling and suggestive of harmony. Critics have often noted the grouping of the figures in threes, as though they were governed by a force which expands from the centre of the composition – Christ – outwards, but returns towards its propelling centre just like a refracted wave – the group of three apostles on Christ's immediate left, with James and

Leonardo, Study for the right arm of Peter. Windsor Castle, Royal Collection (no. 12546)

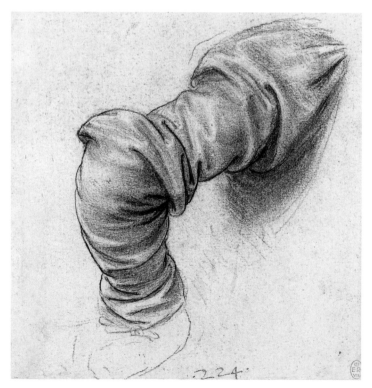

Leonardo, Study for the right foot of Christ. Windsor Castle, Royal Collection (no. 12635r)

Leonardo, Study for the head of Judas. Windsor Castle, Royal Collection (no. 12547)

Thomas leaning towards him. However, this is not the only connecting link between the variety of figures and movements.

The arrangement of the apostles around Christ appears to correspond to a broader, more general plan, in the form of a vast semicircle suggesting an apse. This feeling is conveyed by the greater visual importance of the figures at the ends of the table and the distancing towards deeper planes of the intervening figures. The depth of this great niche seems to be measured by James the Greater's outspread arms and inside it − in a plan it would be a sort of *lunula* − the draped table is exactly placed. Being very long, the table in its turn seems to produce the visual effect of greater height towards the centre, which brings the figure of Christ forward, balancing his backward movement. The disciples thus appear to be arranged like the spokes of a wheel around him, although the axes of the figures present evident variations within this general scheme.

More than in the expressive gestures of the hands, perhaps not altogether free of rhetorical devices, one can note subtle variations in the inclinations of the heads. Only two appear in exact profile, perpendicular to the table − Bartholomew and Matthew, at opposite ends; Simon's head is in *profil perdu,* as though rotating in space, while the others either present a three-quarter view or are slanted with respect to the frontal plane of the painting, in variations that all avoid the orthogonal presentation. Even the second head from the left, which seems to be in profile, should in reality be slightly bent towards the foreground, as can be seen very clearly in the Royal Academy copy (one of the earliest and most faithful). Christ's head, since it emphasizes the vanishing point of the perspective and marks a real spatial depth with respect to the plane of the table, is slightly smaller than the others (about 33 cm high). The heads of the apostles (including those at the ends, Bartholomew and Simon, which appear larger) are all much the same height (36−37 cm approximately). This uniformity in the size of the heads, attenuated however by the foreshortening of those placed obliquely to the plane of the painting, can create a feeling of discomfort, as though they were breaking through towards the frontal plane of the table; for example, the head of Thomas, which should in fact be well back and therefore appear smaller, is larger than Christ's. All this however shows that Leonardo undoubtedly intended to offer a very wide compendium of the *moti dell'anima,* the "movements of the mind" reflected in multiple attitudes and human expressions (his many drawings of caricatural and even "grotesque" heads, where the physiognomical studies are taken to an extreme, probably

Leonardo, central lunette above the Last Supper

derive from his studies for the expressions of the apostles). What other "test," what words other than those pronounced by Christ could so well have illustrated Leonardo's artistic and aesthetic theories? These ideas were explicitly set out in the contemporaneous memorandum of the *Forster Codex* II, ff. 62v-63r[6] and in various notes for the *Treatise on Painting*. There we read, for example: "The movements of men vary with the variety of accidents running through their minds: and each accident in itself moves these men to a greater or lesser degree according to their greater force and age; because the same occurrence will cause a different movement in a young man than in an old one," where the terminology (movements, accidents, greater force, etc.) and the mental process implied are the same applied by Leonardo to the study of the causes of "accidental" or induced movement in mechanics and dynamics.

Assuming that this concatenation of spiritual movements and reactions translated into attitudes and physiognomies is what Leonardo intended to leave to history as the final form of his programmatic manifesto (perfectly matching the visualization of a passage in the Gospels), then the spatial context – the capacity, at first sight rectangular, of the painted refectory in which Jesus and the apostles are sitting – appears as a simple container. The space has been created not so much to give illusory continuity to the real refec-

Leonardo, right and left lunettes above the Last Supper; lunette on the left wall

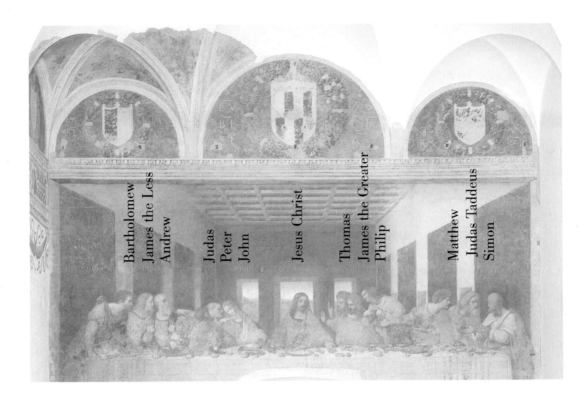

Labels on the image: Bartholomew, James the Less, Andrew, Judas, Peter, John, Jesus Christ, Thomas, James the Greater, Philip, Matthew, Judas Taddeus, Simon

Scheme of the Last Supper

tory (although once that effect must have been much more obvious than today, especially considering the pale tones now emerging and the original lighting of the room),[7] but to accelerate the drama and concentrate the scene on Christ, the main actor in the story unfolding before us. It is Christ who generates all the "movement" in the Leonardian sense ("movement is born of force" — an evident allusion to Christ's spiritual force, remembering the artist's definition: "force is a spiritual virtue"). This clearly foreshadows his later theories referring to the "Prime Mover," God, to which Martin Kemp has recently drawn attention.[8] Christ's word, the Word of God, by giving life to the scene represented, gives life and movement to the whole universe.

After these considerations, the problem of the perspectival construction of the *Cenacolo* appears almost marginal. It may never be finally solved, even after all the incised lines recently discovered in the upper part of the composition[9] have been fully revealed and studied, possibly because it was left deliberately ambiguous by Leonardo himself. He seems to have carefully hidden the few solid reference points which would have allowed a reconstruction of the perspectival scheme (the two painted walls in fact extend beyond the frontal plane of the picture) and has given the room an accelerated perspective rather than the fixed stat-

Facing page
Leonardo, detail of a lunette

*Leonardo, Last Supper, detail
of the apostles on the left*

Leonardo, Last Supper, detail of Christ with the apostles

Leonardo, Last Supper, detail of the apostles on the right

ic perspective of the Florentine tradition, which at that time he was anyway questioning.[10] Rather than the perspectival image of a rectangular room, the result is the contracted image of a trapezoidal container. The problem of perspective cannot in any case be considered separately from the idea and theories relating to the "movements of the mind" which it was Leonardo's chief aim to illustrate, much less be taken as an isolated problem. The architectonic space depicted is used by the artist to test other hypotheses, to check his theories on light and shadow and exemplify them in a form which is in perfect consonance with the diagrams and jottings in the Paris Ms. C.

The painted room behind the apostles is used by Leonardo to experiment with a highly complicated lighting situation. Three different sources of illumination come from the back, mingling like three beams of light shining into an optical box through different openings. And from the left comes a stronger light which Leonardo made more or less coincide with the real light coming through the windows on the left side of the Refectory; finally there is a light coming from the Refectory itself, at right angles – or almost – to the picture plane.

So the wall of the painted room on the left is almost completely in shadow; but towards the vanishing point the shadow should be lessened by the light coming through the windows. The right wall is almost completely illuminated, but the end part is slightly in shadow (a vertical stripe of shade corresponding to the last tapestry in a subtlety which unfortunately has been almost completely lost in the original, but is clearly visible in some copies and even in the Dutertre water-colour). The shadow produced by the part of the back wall beside the first window on the right is lit by the source light which corresponds to that of the real windows. The beautiful drawings of the Paris Ms. C show how behind this differentiated lighting there lie dozens and dozens of studies on proper shadows, "percussed and repercussed," and a passage in f. 14v seems to anticipate the "optical experiment" demonstrated in the *Cenacolo*: "Repercussed shadow is that which is surrounded by lighted wall."

The consonance between what Leonardo has depicted in the *Cenacolo* and his studies of the same period is so exact that I am not convinced, either, by the suggestion that the *Supper* and the gestures of Christ and the apostles should be interpreted as symbolizing the institution of the Eucharist, particularly if this thesis is taken as the sole key to understanding the painting. The moment of the sacrament precedes the revelation of the betrayal and certainly does not demand such an emotional and dramatic reaction as we

see here in the movements and attitudes of the apostles. Saint Mark (14, 22–25) says that: "And as they did eat, Jesus took bread, and blessed, and brake it, and gave to them, and said: "Take, eat: this is my body.' And he took the cup, and when he had given thanks, he gave it to them and they all drank of it. And he said unto them, 'This is my blood...'" In the painting the apostles are neither eating nor drinking nor receiving the blessing, and Christ is not making the gestures described by Saint Mark. Finally, not even Simon's attitude, on the far right, indicates that he is receiving the bread and the wine, as has been claimed after the restoration.[11] Rather than making a "ritual" gesture, he is simply holding out his hands to question, or to question himself without finding an answer ("the other with hands outspread shows their palms... and his mouth expresses amazement" – the description refers to the third apostle from the right, Andrew, but explains his gestures in terms of the astonishment aroused by Christ's words).

Heydenreich accepts the simultaneous existence in the painting of an allusion to the institution of the Eucharist, but considers it a significant addition, and only after having greatly insisted on the fact that the episode depicted by Leonardo is the moment immediately prior to the announcement of the betrayal.[12] Reservations about Steinberg's hypothesis had already been expressed by Anna Maria Brizio.[13]

On the other hand, one simply cannot believe that the scene represents an image blocked like a photogram at a moment which carries a single meaning: the painting is rich with significances and symbolic allusions, and the institution of the Eucharist is one of them. The traditional subject of the *Last Supper* was the most suitable theme to be portrayed in a refectory; but Leonardo, besides the results of more than a decade of studies and experiments, put into it other references and suggestions connected with the Passion of Christ: the offer of self-sacrifice, for example, indicated by the bread and wine, is connected to the *Crucifixion* painted on the opposite wall of the Refectory by Montorfano, and even Christ's position (we should imagine that his feet can be seen, before the door was opened in the wall below) alludes directly to the Crucifixion, with the arms outspread and the feet – as shown in a drawing at Windsor – slightly overlapping. At the same time the bread and the wine, material food for the friars of the Grazie seated at their meal, become their spiritual nourishment after the cycle of the Passion has been completed. Nor can we exclude symbolical meanings in the swags of fruit and leaves which hang above the scene, filling the lunettes. The lunettes are like screens set up between the painted

Leonardo, Last Supper, detail of the table laid for the Last Supper

composition and the real space of the Refectory. They skilfully conceal the point where the wall meets the vaulted ceiling, originally painted in blue with gold stars, which must certainly have created a strong contrast with the illusory coffered ceiling of the mural.

In the central lunette, where the inscription alludes to Ludovico and Beatrice d'Este, dukes of Milan,[14] the garland encloses a coat of arms with contrasting quarters in a chequered pattern. On the dark fields, made of thin silver leaf, the Sforza snakes are painted in bright blue, with typically Leonardesque taste and sensibility. This and the other lunettes were to have been completed by gilding in the ribbons and coats of arms, to strengthen the impression of real shields hanging on the walls (on the opposite wall, the warriors' helmets painted by Montorfano are in relief, simulating metal armour). The garlands as well, particularly the one in the centre, strongly suggest *trompe l'œil*, and their use is certainly connected with the tradition of adorning the fronts of churches and palaces with real wreaths of leaves (as is still done at Easter, for example, on the façade of Saint Mark's in Venice). In Milan it was also custom to decorate palaces with festoons of this sort; Barbara Fabjan has drawn attention to Gian Galeazzo's betrothal to Isabella of Aragon in 1489: the walls of the Castle were adorned with "swags of ivy and laurel made in the antique style" and along the streets were hung "swags of greenery, ornamented with juniper, laurel and ivy," with the ducal insignia. Inside the shield of the coat of arms the recent restoration has

Leonardo, Last Supper,
detail of the face of Christ

revealed the first outline, in the shape of a bucrane. This is the motif used in a drawing at Windsor Royal Library, no. 12282a-r, in a study for a Sforza emblem in Ms. H in Paris, and also in a tondo placed outside the apse of Santa Maria delle Grazie representing another "ducal motif."[15]

The epigraph in the left hand lunette refers to the eldest son, Massimiliano Sforza, in his earldoms of Angera and Pavia,[16] while in the right lunette Ludovico and Beatrice's second son, Francesco II, born in 1495, was to have been celebrated as Duke of Bari; his name however does not appear.[17] The recent restoration indicates that in several points leaves and fruits have been repainted, as can also be deduced from an interesting series of photographs taken by ultraviolet and infrared radiation, a sequence of which is published here. The design is certainly Leonardo's. This is particularly clear in the drawing of the beautiful waving ribbons, a number of lanceolate leaves in the left lunette, the blue snakes already mentioned, and from the general composition. However, the brush stroke seems too heavy and loaded, and the colour in several points is dull despite the exceptionally good state of preservation of the leaves and of several groups of fruit. Nevertheless, laboratory examinations seem to indicate a technique of execution identical with that of the *Cenacolo* below, with the difference that the artist or artists painted (apparently with tempera and an oily binding) directly on a coating of *intonaco*, without the white lead ground used in the *Supper*. The exceptional state of preservation is due to the fact that the lunette paintings

Facing page
Leonardo, Last Supper,
detail of the hands of Philip

were brought to light only in 1854, after four coats of plaster had been removed. According to Ottino Della Chiesa, the lunettes had been subjected to a "ruinous washing,"[18] perhaps in the eighteenth century, and it could therefore be supposed that both the repainting and the subsequent covering over were done at a recent date. However, the decorations seem much earlier; in this case one could suppose that they were covered immediately after the fall of Ludovico il Moro, that is to say after 1499, as a sort of *damnatio memoriae*, to remove the Sforza names and possibly replace them with those of the King of France. It could also be suggested that when Leonardo returned to Milan in 1506, he or one of his pupils reworked the leafy decorations (and certain groups of leaves are stylistically similar to the vegetation that appears in the second version of the *Virgin of the Rocks*), touching up the parts that had fallen or been damaged. It would have to be supposed that the three lunettes were then covered over, since the first mention so far discovered of the existing decorations dates back only to Giuseppe Mazza, in 1770.[19]

In Northern Italian painting, as well, motifs of swags and garlands had a long and illustrious tradition: we need only recall Mantegna's decorations in the Camera degli Sposi at Mantua, or paintings by Carlo Crivelli such as the *Madonna della Candeletta* in the Brera Gallery. Leonardo's choice of this motif is therefore not surprising; and his interest in vegetation is testified by a large number of extremely sensitive botanical drawings which show his extraordinary perceptiveness in rendering the world of plants. The first two lunettes of the long walls in the Refectory also seem to have been decorated by Leonardo. Only the brush drawing in the first lunette on the west wall survives (the one on the east side was destroyed, together with the whole wall, in the 1943 bombing). After its recent cleaning Carlo Bertelli confirmed it as an autograph drawing.[20]

It is correct to suppose that Leonardo began working on the preparatory studies for the *Cenacolo* in the first half of the final decade of the fifteenth century. The enlargement and decoration of the Refectory of the Grazie was part of a wider programme designed to celebrate the Sforza dynasty and Ludovico il Moro in particular. The new apse of the church, built to Bramante's design from 1492 onwards, was the most important and significant work executed in this context. Intended to hold the tombs of Ludovico and his wife by Cristoforo Solari, now preserved in the Certosa of Pavia, the monumental complex must have appeared as a sort of mausoleum, invested with theological and religious meanings beyond its symbolic and celebrative purpose.[21]

The contribution by Bramante and Leonardo to this gener-

Leonardo, Last Supper, detail of the figure of Andrew

Leonardo, Last Supper, detail of the figure of Judas

al programme are further connected by assonances between the architectural ideals expressed by Bramante and the new, monumental scale adopted by Leonardo for the figures of the *Supper* which also seems to refer to an architectural, or even directly Bramantesque idea (compare the figure of Simon with those of the *Men at Arms* of Casa Panigarola, now at Brera). The illusionistic motif of Leonardo's painted architecture recalls Bramante's fake choir in the church of San Satiro, although the blatantly scenographic intentions of the later are, as we have seen, ultimately a secondary purpose in Leonardo's mural. And in 1495 Donato Montorfano had finished his *Crucifixion* on the wall opposite to the *Cenacolo*, although this seems to have been commissioned by the Dominican friars of Santa Maria delle Grazie.

Ludovico il Moro's personal interest in Leonardo's *Supper* is attested by a letter to Marchesino Stanga asking the latter to solicit the artist "so that he may finish the work begun in the Refectory of the Grazie and subsequently attend to another wall of this Refectory." The letter, dated 29 June 1497,[22] besides providing supporting evidence for the idea that Leonardo was also commissioned to decorate the wall that Montorfano had finished painting only two years earlier, also gives a first chronological peg for the conclusive phase of Leonardo's work. The *Last Supper* was certainly finished in the following year, 1498, as Luca Pacioli states in the famous passage, already quoted, from his *De divina proportione*.[23] To date the beginning, one must remember that time was certainly needed to work out the theme and we know nothing of the intermediate drawings between the early studies of the Windsor sheet, already discussed, and the drawings of the apostles's heads, which belong to the final stage of preparation. This, and even more the painting technique chosen by Leonardo (not *buon fresco*, which would have required a rapid, immediate execution, but a technique which would allow him to add further touches later, as Matteo Bandello recalls in his famous story)[24] indicate a year around 1494, if not earlier, as the starting date for his work in the Refectory.[25]

The scientific observations and theoretical notes on painting which I have quoted are from manuscripts datable between 1490 and 1494, which seems to confirm this chronology. Moreover, insufficient attention is usually given to Bandello's testimony as an element for dating the *Cenacolo*. Speaking of how Leonardo often went to the Grazie to paint the *Supper*, he refers to the equestrian monument to Francesco Sforza: "I have also seen him, according to how the caprice or impulse took him, set out at midday, when the sun is in Leo, from the Corte Vecchia where that marvellous clay horse stood, and come straight to the Gra-zie and, climbing on the scaffolding, take the brush and give a few strokes to one of the figures, then immediately leave and go elsewhere."

It would be very interesting if we could establish what stage of the Sforza monument Bandello is alluding to, since we know that Leonardo had returned to his studies for the horse in 1490 (after probably starting on the project in 1482–83), while the *Codex 8937* of the Biblioteca Nacional of Madrid mentions the final studies for a second version, the finishing of a clay model and, finally, the relative cast-ing in 1493: "20th of December 1493... I finished casting the horse without the tail and on its side." In order for the horse to be cast, however, the clay model must have been finished some time earlier, because in the revolutionary method invented by Leonardo the wax model was to be ob-tained from the clay model piece by piece.[26] It must be not-ed that according to Bandello, Leonardo was working si-multaneously on the clay model and the *Cenacolo*; since work on the "great horse" seems to have been stopped dur-ing 1494–95 ("I will say nothing of the horse because I know the times")[27] and since the "few strokes" Bandello talks about can only refer to a very advanced stage of the work of the *Supper*, we must suppose that Bandello was referring to a period closer to 1492–93 than 1494–95 (a remark about the Cardinal of Gurk's visit, which took place in 1497, precedes Bandello's mention of the clay model for the horse, but this cannot be used to date his description of Leonardo's habits).

Only twenty years after it had been completed, the painting already began to deteriorate: Antonio de Beatis, who visit-ed the *Supper* in 1517–18, found it "very excellent, al-though it is beginning to be spoiled, due either to the dumpness of the wall or to some other accident."[28] Fifty years later the situation must have become much more serious, creating the mistaken idea that the cause of the decay was an imperfect execution. The Aretine Vasari does not fail to say this spitefully, stating that the work "was so badly done that nothing can be seen any more but a faded smudge."[29] Lomazzo tries to improve matters and justify the master by affirming that the painting was done in oil on an unsuitable *imprimitura*. With Armenini, who found it "half spoiled although most beautiful" we see the beginning of a fashion for decaying masterpieces foreshadowing the Romantic ideal. Subsequent judgements, from Scannelli's (1642) to the accounts by Lattuada (1738), de Brosses (1738), Bartoli (1776) and Domenico Pino (1796), are interlaced with criticisms and problems of methodology raised by the first documented attempts at "restoration," by

Michelangelo Bellotti in 1726 and Giuseppe Mazza in 1770 (although it is not impossible that traces of earlier interventions may be found).

The first intervention was alternately praised and criticized (particularly by Bianconi, 1787) because Bellotti did a number of reworkings in tempera or gouache and revarnished the whole wall in oil (this at least hiding the original painting under his interventions, which however seem to have spared the figures of Judas, Peter, John and Christ). Mazza set himself to remove Bellotti's repainting, using a scraper and filling in the gaps with an oil mixture, particularly on Bartholomew and, to a lesser extent, on James and Andrew.[30]

A careful inspection carried out by Andrea Appiani in 1802 identified the dampness of the wall as the cause of the fall of painting and recognized the impossibility of transferring the mural altogether. In 1821 Stefano Barezzi made an attempt, limited to the area of the tablecloth under the figures of Bartholomew and Christ, to see whether a transfer could in fact be made by consolidating the painting with glue and adding coloured waxbased stuccoes. In 1853–55 Barezzi intervened on the whole surface, consolidating and cleaning it (it was Barezzi, as already mentioned, who removed the plaster concealing the decorations in the lunettes).

A publication by Pinin Brambilla Barcilon shows some remarkable photographs of these early interventions: one can see Bellotti's repainting of Thaddeus' eyes and the tablecloth decorations, and Barezzi's incisions on the table and the flattened picture surface in the areas where he tried to strip off the painting, areas which were then filled with a wax-based material.[31]

The restorations of this century, finally done using physical analyses of the environmental conditions and the chemical components of the painting, allowed the picture to be consolidated as far as possible. Cavenaghi in 1908 established that the *Cenacolo* had been executed in tempera on two layers of preparation. Silvestri, in 1924, did a new cleaning and a new consolidation (applying plaster round the edges of the painted ground). After the bombing of 1943 and the consequent reconstruction of the Refectory east wall, it seemed that every preceding effort to preserve the mural had been in vain. So much dust and condensed humidity was produced by the rebuilding of the wall and floor that Wittgens found the painting darkened and dimmed: "Instead of somewhat white, it appeared completely black... the surface of the *Cenacolo*, swollen with humidity, looked like a rubbery fabric and at the least touch not only the paint but also the underlying chalk priming came away..."[32]

Ettore Modigliani, the Superintendent of the time, therefore invited Mauro Pelliccioli to attempt a new consolidation of the painting surface, "to be done more radically than the previous work by Cavenaghi and Silvestri." In 1947 Pelliccioli began to fix the flakes of paint to the plaster by brushing on de-waxed shellac dissolved in alcohol and injecting casein behind it. The shellac gave the paint cohesion, consistency and a lively colour again, so it was possible to go on to the next stage. In 1951–52 and 1954 Pelliccioli worked at recovering Leonardo's original painting. Wittgens pointed out early on that Pelliccioli had intervened particularly where "the eighteenth century colours had hidden the brilliant treasure of Leonardo's own painting." Pelliccioli's cautious and limited cleaning, while achieving extraordinary recoveries – the Assisi embroidery on the tablecloth, the blue of Judas' robe decorated with Cufic letters in gold – stopped short of removing all the old repainting. Pinin Brambilla remarks that "one notes a greater care, in fact, to remove the repainting on the flesh, while the reworking of the eyes and the dark outlines round the faces and hands remain, and he has not insisted on removing the stratifications deposited on the abrasions or in the gaps to avoid making the picture unintelligible."[33] On entire areas, therefore, the repainting was not removed, including the coffered ceiling, the walls with tapestries and the part below the table.

The restoration which has just been finished, was made necessary by a worsening of the environmental conditions of the Refectory and the wall during the sixties and seventies, when a thick layer of dust and smog was deposited on the painting. Preliminary examinations for a new cleaning were begun in 1976 under the guidance of the Soprintendenza per i Beni Artistici e Storici di Milano, then directed by Franco Russoli. He was succeeded by Stella Matalon, Carlo Bertelli, Rosalba Tardito and Pietro Petraroia (since 1993 with my collaboration) who have been supported by the skill of Pinin Brambilla Barcilon. Thanks to the progress of scientific and technical knowledge, it has been possible to make analyses and examinations covering the chemical, physical, environmental, static, structural, and climatic conditions, besides an exhaustive and detailed photographic documentation.[34] This work has been done under the supervision of the Istituto Centrale del Restauro. At the same time a restoration methodology has been perfected and applied which aimed to recover all that remains of Leonardo's own painting, removing the repaintings, old and new, which have to a large extent concealed it up to now. The sections that were repainted have not, however, all been removed. The coffered ceiling remains an eigh-

teenth-century reworking (although a small section of the original has been brought to light on the right), and so do the tapestries, however, on the left, under the heavy eighteenth-century repainting, bunches of flowers belonging to the original design were found. The very damaged head of Judas has been left in its eighteenth-century form, though recent layers of colour have been removed and it has been rendered closer to the original profile. However, this was not a purely aesthetic criterion of restoration: the repaintings, the layers of grime, the mould, the different materials accumulated over the painting during the centuries, have threatened the complex and already delicate mechanical situation produced from the outset by Leonardo's choice of technique. Problems include areas of cleavage, the fall of flakes of paint and ground, and variable reactions of humidity and heat.

The courageous pursuit of this restoration methodology has permitted the recovery of pictorial fragments that, for the very first time, enable us to see Leonardo's "original" painting (though in a fragmentary state of preservation that has been jeopardized by the nine previous restorations) and, in particular, his colours.[35] The figure of Simon on the extreme right has regained its volume and monumentality (closer to Bramante than to Michelangelo) and its iridescent lilac and white tones. Fully revealed in Matthew are the noble profile and wave of emotion pervading him, and the intense, brilliant blue of his tunic. Other elements which have emerged are the grieved but not pathetic expression of Philip, and the deep plasticity of James the Greater's face in its three quarter view with the repressed sigh of amazement that seems to issue from his mouth, with none of the caricatural emphasis of the corresponding Windsor drawing. After dwelling on these portions of the painting — which, though only a few surviving fragments, are of an extremely high quality and imbued with an astonishing light that seems to regenerate even the surrounding areas where only the ground appears — and observing the parts on the left where the heads of Bartholomew, Andrew, Peter and John have been restored (nearly all of them had been enlarged and distorted by previous repainting), the meticulous work, which has "freed" the painting that was bridled, almost obscured, by previous reworking, is clearly evident. The beautiful heads of Bartholomew and James the Less — almost ancient profiles — have been restored to their original design and part of their former beauty, and act as a counterpoint to that of Matthew.

[1] Cf. K. Clark, *The Drawings of Leonardo da Vinci in the Collection of Her Majesty the Queen at Windsor Castle*, second edition revised with the assistance of C. Pedretti, London 1968–69, vol. I, pp. 99–100.

[2] Cf. J. Wasserman, "Reflections on the Last Supper of Leonardo da Vinci," in *Arte Lombarda*, 66, no. 3, 1983, p. 19–20, figs. 6–8.

[3] Among the other preparatory studies, there are the sheets from Windsor Royal Library, nos. 12551 and 12552 (the heads of Philip and James the Greater), 12546 (Peter's right arm), 12543 (John's hands) and 12635r (Christ's feet); doubts have been raised concerning the autography of sheets no. 12547 (Judas' head, which however it seems should be considered authentic), 12548 (the head of Bartholomew or, according to Berenson, that of Matthew; the drawing is almost universally accepted as an original; the doubts about the autography have been raised recently by Carlo Pedretti), 12549 and 12550 (which are in fact copies after a drawing by Leonardo for the head of Simon), 12544 and 12545 (copies of drawings for the hands of Matthew and Thomas). For all these sheets, cf. K. Clark, *op. cit.*, pp. 100–2 and 133, and for other related studies, see the recent catalogue by C. Pedretti, *Leonardo - Studi per il Cenacolo*, Milan 1983, *passim*. Amongst the preparatory drawings for the *Last Supper*, I do not consider the sheet in the Accademia of Venice suspected of being a counterfeit (cf. A.M. Brizio, "Lo studio degli Apostoli nella Cena dell'Accademia di Venezia," in *Raccolta Vinciana*, XVIII, 1959, p. 45 ff., and XX, 1964, p. 414) although when recent opinions seem to rehabilitate it (cf. C. Pedretti, *Leonardo da Vinci inedito - Tre saggi*, Florence 1968, pp. 56–60; Luisa Cogliati Arano had accepted it as a counterfeit in her catalogue of the Venice drawings in 1966, but now seems uncertain: cf. L. Cogliati Arano, *I disegni di Leonardo e della sua cerchia alla Gallerie dell'Accademia*, Milan 1980, pp. 56–57). The drawing was probably begun by Leonardo, who wrote in the names of the apostles himself, but has been largely reworked by a Milanese artist who was much less skilled than the master. A comparison suggests itself with the famous drawing of the *Head of Christ* at the Pinacoteca di Brera, recently proposed again as an original drawing by Leonardo subsequently altered by one or more hands (cf. P.C.

Marani, in D*isegni lombardi del Cinque e Seicento della Pinacoteca di Brera e dell'Arcivescovado*, Florence 1986, pp. 27–31).

[4] Cf. P.C. Marani, "Leonardo dalla scienza all'arte" - Un cambiamento di stile, gli antefatti, una cronologia," in *Fra Rinascimento, manierismo e realtà - Scritti di storia dell'arte in memoria di Anna Maria Brizio*, Florence 1984, p. 44.

[5] Published by A.M. Brizio, *Scritti scelti di Leonardo da Vinci*, Turin 1952 (1966 edition, pp. 252–54).

[6] Cf. J.P. Richter, *The Literary Works of Leonardo da Vinci*, Oxford 1883 (1970 edition, paragraphs 665 and 666).

[7] The theory that the stationary point chosen by Leonardo for the perspectival construction of the *Supper* coincides with the real view of the spectator has been abandoned after the discovery that, in reality, the perspectival point of view is situated about four metres above the original level of the floor of the room. For the most recent studies on the perspective of the *Cenacolo*, see the bibliographical note added to the new edition of A.M. Brizio, *Leonardo da Vinci - Il Cenacolo*, Florence 1983.

[8] M. Kemp, *Leonardo da Vinci - The Marvellous Works of Nature and Man*, London 1981, pp. 261–329.

[9] Carlo Bertelli mentions it in the first reports of the restoration in progress: cf. note 35.

[10] On Leonardo's recovery of mediaeval optics, see the fundamental essay by A.M. Brizio, *Razzi incidenti e razzi refressi (III Lettura vinciana)*, Florence 1963.

[11] C. Bertelli, in L.H. Heydenreich, *Invito a Leonardo - L'Ultima Cena*, Milan 1982, p. 8. The thesis according to which Leonardo depicted the institution of the Eucharist goes back to von Einem and has been more recently reproposed by L. Steinberg. This thesis is rejected by others, including A. Ottino Della Chiesa (*L'opera completa di Leonardo pittore*, Milan 1967, p. 8), who usefully draws attention to a passage by Pacioli in his *De divina proportione*: "It is impossible to imagine the Apostles more attentively alive to the sound of the voice of the ineffable truth when it spoke: 'Unus vestrum me traditurus est.' With actions and gestures from one to another, with vivid and pained amazement they seem to speak to each other, so nobly did our Leonardo arrange them with his graceful hand" (1498). To this should be added the earliest engravings, attrib-

uted to Zoan Andrea or to the Master of the Sforza Book of Hours, where the words with which Christ announces the betrayal appear in a label (one of these engravings is reproduced, for example, by L.H. Heydenreich, *op. cit.*, p. 103; others in C. Alberici, M. Chirico De Biasi, *Leonardo e l'incisione*, Milan 1984, pp. 59–61).

[12] L.H. Heydenreich, *op. cit.*, pp. 41–48.

[13] A.M. Brizio, "Il Cenacolo," in *Leonardo - La pittura*, Florence 1977, pp. 106–107.

[14] The inscription "LV[dovicus] MA[ria] BE[atrix] EST[ensis] SF[ortia] AN[glus] DVX [Mediolani]" now appears in white beside the arms and the garland, against the red ground of the priming.

[15] Cf. C. Pedretti, *op. cit.*, pp. 86–91.

[16] "MA[ria] M[a]X[imilianus] SF[ortia] AN[glus] CO[mes] P[a]P[iae]."

[17] "SF[ortia] AN[glus] DVX BARI." Francesco II received the title of Duke of Bari in 1497. This date is generally taken as an inclusive limit for dating the lunettes, which are therefore traditionally supposed to have been executed between 1495 (birth of the second son) and 1497 (bestowal of the title of Duke of Bari). This dating put forward for the lunettes does not however contradict what is said further on about the possibility of anticipating the date of the beginning of the *Cenacolo*.

[18] A. Ottino Della Chiesa, *op. cit.*, p. 99.

[19] Cf. B. Fabjan, "Il Cenacolo nuovamente restaurato," in *Leonardo - La pittura*, Florence 1985, p. 93, note 1.

[20] C. Bertelli, *op. cit.*, pp. 12 and 145 (plate).

[21] See the essay by S. Lang "Leonardo's Architectural Designs and the Sforza Mausoleum," in *Journal of the Warburg and Courtauld Institutes*, vol. XXXI, 1968, pp. 218–33. Also see M. Rossi, "Novità per Santa Maria delle Grazie di Milano," in *Arte Lombarda*, 66, 1983, pp. 35–70, and for other connections, P.C. Marani, "Leonardo e le colonne 'ad tronchonos' - Tracce di un programma iconologico per Ludovico il Moro," in *Raccolta Vinciana*, XXI, 1982, pp. 103–20.

[22] The letter is quoted in its entirety in almost all the literature on the *Cenacolo*: see in L. Beltrami, *Documenti e memorie riguardanti la vita e le opere di Leonardo da Vinci*, Milan 1919, pp. 48–49.

[23] Cf. above, note 12.

[24] M. Bandello, *Le novelle*, Bari 1910, vol. II, p. 283.

[25] The Leonardo passage from the Paris Ms. H, f. 64, dated 29 January 1494, presented recently also by L.H. Hey-

denreich (*op. cit.*, p. 32, n. 3) in support of a proposal to date the commission of the *Cenacolo* to 1494, is not probatory, however. In fact, "il pian delle mura," "la sala" and "la ghirlanda" of which Leonardo speaks refer not to the *Cenacolo* but to the Castle of Milan. The correction was recently made by Pedretti, *op. cit.*, p. 70, independently, by P.C. Marani, *L'architettura fortificata negli studi di Leonardo da Vinci, con il catalogo completo dei disegni*, Florence 1984, pp. 139–40.

[26] On the "Sforza horse," cf. M.V. Brugnoli, "Il monumento Sforza," in *Leonardo*, edited by L. Reti, Milan 1974, pp; 86–109.

[27] The mention occurs in a draft letter to Ludovico il Moro in which reference is also made to the commission "to paint the small rooms" in the Castle and which Brizio places before a text of the Paris Ms. H dated 1494. Cf. A.M. Brizio, *op. cit.*, 1952 (1966, pp. 639–40).

[28] L. Pastor, *Die Reise dess Cardinals Luigi d'Aragona*, Freiburg 1905.

[29] G. Vasari, *Le vite de' più eccellenti pittori scultori e architetti*, Florence 1568.

[30] For this and the following information, cf. B. Fabjan, *op. cit.*, p. 93 ff., note 1.

[31] P. Brambilla Barcilon, *Il Cenacolo di Leonardo in Santa Maria delle Grazie - Storia, condizioni, problemi*, Milan 1985, fig. 1, pp. 15–19.

[32] F. Wittgens, "Restauro del Cenacolo," in *Leonardo - Saggi e ricerche*, edited by the "Comitato Nazionale per le Onoranze a Leonardo da Vinci nel quinto centenario della nascita," Rome 1954, pp. 3–4.

[33] P. Brambilla Barcilon, *op. cit.*, p. 66.

[34] See, for example, the report by the Istituto Centrale del Restauro in Rome, dated 20 September 1977; the report by H. Travers Newton of 10 September 1977; the thermohygrometric tests by the Centro "Gino Bozza" of Milan in September 1979; the tests for the pollution of the air in the room of the *Cenacolo* conducted by the Stazione Sperimentale per i Combustibili, Milan, on 18 October 1979, etc., all in Soprintendenza per i Beni Artistici e Storici di Milano, Archivio corrente, 13/31. See also M. Matteini, A. Moles, "A Preliminary Investigation of the Unusual Technique of Leonardo's Mural 'The Last Supper', in *Studies in Conservation*, 24, 1979, pp. 125–33, and the analyses published in *Arte Lombarda*, 62, 1982. Cf. also H. Travers Newton, "Leonardo da Vinci as Mural Painters: Some Observations on His Materials and Working Methods," in *Arte Lombarda*, 66, 1983, pp. 71–88.

[35] See the reports on the first sensational discoveries: C. Bertelli, B. Fabjan, "Il Cenacolo di Leonardo," in *Brera-Notizie della Pinacoteca*, autumn-winter 1981–82, pp. 1–4; C. Bertelli, *op. cit.*, pp. 127–56; C. Bertelli, "Il Cenacolo vinciano," in *Santa Maria delle Grazie*, Milan 1983, pp. 188–95; D.A. Brown, *Leonardo's Last Supper: The Restoration*, Washington D.C. 1983; B. Fabjan, *op. cit.*, pp. 90–94. See also C. Bertelli, "Verso il vero Leonardo," in *Leonardo e Milano*, edited by G.A. Dell'Acqua, Milan 1982, pp. 83–88.

Bibliography

Accounts of the restoration work as it proceeded from top to bottom and right to left, further to the above-mentioned studies, have been given by: P. Brambilla Barcilon, *Il Cenacolo di Leonardo...*, cit., 1984; B. Fabjan in *Leonardo. La pittura*, 1985, pp. 90 94; C. Bertelli, "Leonardo e l'Ultima Cena (c. 1595–97)," in *Tecnica e stile: esempi di pittura murale del Rinascimento italiano*, eds. E. Borsook and F. Superbi Gioffredi, The Harvard University Center for Italian Renaissance Studies at Villa I Tatti, Florence 1986, pp. 31–42; P. C. Marani, "Leonardo's Last Supper: Some Problems of Restoration and New Light on Leonardo's Art," in *Nine Lectures on Leonardo da Vinci*, eds. A. Bednarek and F. Ames Lewis, University of London, London 1990, pp. 45–52; id., "Le alterazioni dell'immagine dell'Ultima Cena di Leonardo dopo le più recenti analisi," in *Kermès. Arte e tecnica del restauro*, III, no. 7, 1990, pp. 64–67; R. Tardito, "Il Cenacolo di Leonardo e il suo recente restauro," in *Raccolta Vinciana*, XXIII, 1989, pp. 3–16; P. Brambilla Barcilon and P.C. Marani, "Le lunette di Leonardo nel Refettorio delle Grazie," in *Quaderni del Restauro*, 7, 1990.

A first photographic report on the righthand section of the composition after its restoration (including the figure of Christ) is published in P.C. Marani, *Leonardo*, Milan 1994 (other editions: Madrid 1995; Paris 1996). The analyses carried out during the recent restoration work have brought to light the medium adopted by Leonardo: tempera (perhaps mixed with oil) applied to two layers of base, the first thicker layer of calcium carbonate, the second thinner layer to which the paint was applied of white lead. See H. Kuhn, "Bericht über die Naturwissenschaftliche Untersuchungen der Malerei des Mailänder Abendmahls," in *Maltechnik*, IV. 1985, pp. 24–51. The most important analyses carried out on the mural painting, the physical and chemical results, and the precautions taken for its conservation will soon be published in a volume edited by G. Basile and M. Marabelli, *Il Cenacolo di Leonardo. Analisi e ricerche*, Milan, 1999. The final report on the restoration and the resulting new information are contained in P.C. Marani and P. Brambilla Barcilon, *Leonardo. L'Ultima Cena*, Milan 1999.

The restoration that has now been completed and began with cleaning attempts in 1977 has raised some comments and criticism. The most serious comes from M. Kemp, "Looking at Leonardo's Last Supper," in *Appearance, Opinion, Change: Evaluating the Look of Paintings*, United Institute for Conservation, London 1990, and "Authentically Dirty Pictures," in *The Times Literary Supplement*, 17 May 1991, to whom P.C. Marani replied in "Lettera a Martin Kemp (sul restauro del Cenacolo," in *Raccolta Vinciana*, XXV, 1993, pp. 463–67. M. Kemp replied to this in "Letter to Pietro Marani (on the restoration of the Last Supper)," in *Raccolta Vinciana*, XXVI, 1995, pp. 359–66. See also J. Franck, "The Last Supper, 1497–1997: The Moment of Truth," in *Academia Leonardi Vinci. Journal of Leonardo Studies and Bibliography of Vinciana*, vol. X, 1997, pp. 165–82.

P.C.M.

The South Wall

Giovanni Donato Montorfano

Crucifixion
1495

On the wall opposite Leonardo's *Last Supper* there is the vast composition frescoed by Donato Montorfano, which extends into the spaces of the lunettes. The presence of a *Crucifixion* and a *Last Supper* on the two shorter walls of monastery refectories is a widespread tradition, and the two large mural paintings were executed almost at the same time. However, the importance of Leonardo's masterpiece tends to make one "forget" this less advanced though interesting *Crucifixion*. The scene, rich in figures and descriptive detail, is in a far better state of preservation than Leonardo's painting. Unlike Leonardo, Montorfano adopted the traditional fresco technique which is more durable and long lasting. The comparison is rendered even more evident by the now extremely faint portraits of the family of Ludovico il Moro added in *secco* on the edges of the painting, next to the groups of Dominican saints.
The date 1495 and Montorfano's signature are clearly visible on a stone at Mary Magdelen's feet, beneath the cross. This is the only work signed and dated by the artist, who painted it at the end of his career. The composition reflects the tradition of the Lombard school and the figures are arranged in groups around three very tall crosses. Note particularly, on the left, the closeknit group formed by the women supporting Mary, a theme that frequently recurs in fifteenth century Lombard painting and sculpture, and that also appears in the *Crucifixion* by Bramantino in the Pinacoteca di Brera. The walled city of Jerusalem can be seen in the background, against a rocky landscape that reflects Paduan influences.
The buildings display "modern" architectural features, and are almost a tribute to the style of Bramante, with whom Donato Montorfano was in direct contact.

Photo credits
Archivio Electa, Milano
Antonio Quattrone, Firenze
© The Royal Collection,
Her Majesty Queen Elisabeth II,
Windsor

This volume was printed by Elemond S.p.A.
at the plant in Martellago (Venice) in 1999